Test Your Maths 8

Years 8 – 10

CORONEOS PUBLICATIONS

Item No 570

This book is available from recognised booksellers or contact:

Coroneos Publications

Telephone: (02) 9838 9265   **Facsimile:** (02) 9838 8982
Business Address: 2/195 Prospect Highway Seven Hills 2147
Website: www.coroneos.com.au
E-mail: info@fivesenseseducation.com.au

Item # 570
Test Your Maths 8
by Frank & Valerie Marett
First published 2019

ISBN: 978-1-922034-79-3
© Frank & Valerie Marett

Test Your Maths 8

How to Use This Book
Score each page. Write the scores in the box. Mark as you go.

Each section indicates skills passed or failed. Answers are at the back of the book. <u>Complete one section at a time.</u> Your child may <u>not</u> use a calculator.

Do not help your child. <u>Do not proceed to the next section if your child has failed to gain the required score.</u>

Instructions on how to use the scores to discover which books are necessary to improve your child's knowledge are given on the next page.

<u>It is considered essential that children pass certain tests. Read the results carefully to ensure you know which tests are involved and what you can do to rectify any problems.</u>

1	2	3	4	5	6	7	8	9
10	11	12	13	14	15	16	17	18
19	20	21	22	23	24	25	26	27
28	29	30	31	32	33	34	35	36
37	38	39	40	41	42	43	44	45
46	47	48	49	50	51	52	53	54

Score: /922
Pass: 688/922

To assess results go to page 2.

Overall Score

Above 688

Proceed to *Maths Revision & Practice 3 & 4*, then *Understanding Maths 9 & 10*.

510 - 688

Work through *Maths Revision & Practice 2* and *Understanding Maths 8*.

344 - 510

Go back to *Maths Revision & Practice* and *Understanding Maths 7*.

Below 344

Go back to *Easy-learn 4A & Easy-learn Maths 4B* then continue sequentially.

Essential Knowledge

Tests 1-18

If your child can not pass these pages with at least a 70% pass you need to go back to Easy Learn Maths 4B and 5A and then proceed sequentially. This is foundational work. It is impossible to just fill in the gaps and proceed from this point. Maths is used in:

- **Addition, subtraction, multiplication** and **division** are used in every aspect of our lives.

- **Fractions:** apart from being an essential component of every day living, e.g., cooking, a student can not work on algebra until they understand fractions thoroughly.

- **Percentages:** our banking system is built on an understanding of the percentage that will be paid to you on your savings and the percentage you pay to the bank on the money borrowed. Without this knowledge an adult will not be well equipped financially.

- **Decimals:** Australian society and industry is based on the decimal system. We use it when we use money, measuring, banking, statistics, science etc. It is an essential foundation of our society. A student without this knowledge is ill-equipped to cope with life in the adult world.

Basic Knowledge on the following begins:

Fractions: *Easy-learn 4B*

Area & Perimeter: *Easy-learn 4B*

Angles: *Easy-learn 4B*

Volume: *Easy-learn 5B*

Decimals: *Easy-learn 5B*

Averages: *Easy-learn 5B*

Long Division: *Easy-learn 6A*

Geometry—angles, triangles: *Easy-learn 6A*

Percentages: *Easy-learn 6B*

Test 1: Adding & Subtracting

A. Solve the following addition and subtractions. (1 point each)

1.	4517 +1382	4638 +4692	8344 +4915	6828 + 7498	8425 +2488
2.	9456 - 3813	8245 - 3486	9898 - 4945	7275 - 3838	6668 - 2894
3.	8724 - 3818	9974 - 4965	7868 - 2834	4296 - 1632	6888 - 5559
4.	9570 +7372	8689 + 5432	7834 +6691	7688 + 7596	8227 +3487
5.	5876 + 9845	7460 - 5729	6176 + 6467	9949 - 7642	1583 - 631
6.	7544 + 6497	9766 - 3594	8667 +5688	9294 - 3765	1782 +1279

B. Answer the following problems. (1 point each)

1. 8,000 + 3,000 - 2,000 = _____

2. 15,000 + 13,000 - 12,000 = _____

3. 28,480 - 2,440 + 27,250 = _____

4. 52, 760 - 23, 940 - 5,444 = _____

Score: /34

Pass: 25 /34

Australian Homeschooling #570
Test Your Maths 8

Test 2: Long Division

Answer questions. Do not use a calculator. (2 points each question)

1.
$$28 \overline{)4368}$$

2.
$$17 \overline{)4131}$$

3.
$$57 \overline{)5073}$$

4.
$$23 \overline{)9706}$$

5.
$$13 \overline{)1261}$$

6.
$$35 \overline{)595}$$

7.
$$46 \overline{)1702}$$

8.
$$99 \overline{)12177}$$

9.
$$21 \overline{)483}$$

Score: /18

14/18

Test 3: Long Multiplication

Answer questions. Do not use a calculator. (2 points each question.)

1.
```
    27
X  35
_____
```

2.
```
   482
X 124
_____
```

3.
```
    37
X  96
_____
```

4.
```
   123
X 223
_____
```

5.
```
    78
X  17
_____
```

6.
```
    42
X  89
_____
```

7.
```
    32
X  99
_____
```

8.
```
    72
X  68
_____
```

9.
```
   376
X   19
_____
```

Score: /18

Pass: 14/18

© Valerie Marett
Coroneos Publications

Australian Homeschooling #570
Test Your Maths 8

Test 4: Fractions

A. Reduce the fraction to its simplest form (1 point each answer)

1. 9/12 _____
2. 4/28 _____
3. 6/12 _____

4. 5/20 _____
5. 14/21 _____
6. 30/36 _____

7. 6/18 _____
8. 56/64 _____
9. 18/36 _____

10. 45/80 _____
11. 20/48 _____
12. 10/35 _____

B. Equivalent fractions (1 point each answer)

1. 5/20 = 1/? = _____
2. 4/6 = 2/? = _____

3. 9/12 = 3/? = _____
4. 50/100 = 1/? _____

5. 15/25 = 3/? = _____
6. 3/21 = 1/? _____

C. Express as a whole number (1 point each answer)

1. 110/55 = _____
2. 15/3 = _____
3. 36/9 = _____

4. 51/3 = _____
5. 96/8 = _____
6. 55/11 = _____

7. 125/25 = _____
8. 45/5 = _____
9. 56/8 = _____

D. Express as a mixed number (1 point each answer)

1. 22/3 = _____
2. 33/8 = _____
3. 68/9 = _____

4. 17/2 = _____
5. 15/4 = _____
6. 87/4 = _____

Score: _____/33

25/33

© Valerie Marett
Coroneos Publications

Australian Homeschooling #570
Test Your Maths 8

Test 5: Addition of Fractions

A. Add the following fractions. (1 point each)

1. $1/3 + 2/3 =$ _____

2. $5/9 + 1/3 =$ _____

3. $3/5 + 3/10: =$ _____

4. $7/12 + 1/2 =$ _____

5. $7/14 + 4/7 =$ _____

6. $1/2 + 9/3 =$ _____

7. $7/15 + 2/5 =$ _____

8. $5/2 + 1/8 =$ _____

B. Add the following mixed numbers. (1 point each)

1. $5\,7/12 + 3/4 =$ _____

2. $16/33 + 4\,1/11 =$ _____

3. $1\,3/5 + 5\,3/7 =$ _____

4. $9\,5/12 + 1\,11/2 =$ _____

5. $5\,2/9 + 3/10: =$ _____

6. $2\,4/5 + 4\,1/3 =$ _____

7. $9/21 + 5\,6/7 =$ _____

8. $5\,25/20 + 4\,1/2 =$ _____

Score: /16

13/16

Test 6: Subtraction of Fractions

A. Subtract the following fractions. (1 point each)

1. 1/4 - 2/9 = _____

2. 8/9 - 3/11 = _____

3. 3/5 - 3/8 = _____

4. 7/12 - 1/2 = _____

5. 33/40 - 3/10: = _____

6. 3/2 - 1/2 = _____

7. 6/2 - 4/5 = _____

8. 1/3 - 2/9 = _____

B. Subtract the following mixed numbers. (1 point each)

1. 6 1/2 - 4 2/3 = _____

2. 9 3/4 - 8 1/3 = _____

3. 2 1/12 - 2/3 = _____

4. 2 5/8 - 2 1/4 = _____

5. 5 1/2 - 3 3/8 = _____

6. 9 5/18 - 2 1/9 = _____

7. 8 4/8 - 1 2/3 = _____

8. 7 5/9 - 5 10/27 = _____

Score: /16

12/16

8

Test 7: Addition and Subtraction of Fractions

A. Calculate the value of following fractions. (1 point each)

1. $1/3 + 2/3 + 2/3 =$ _____

2. $1/9 + 1/12 + 9/15 =$ _____

3. $10/20 - 6/30 + 5/10: =$ _____

4. $7/18 - 4/9 + 2/3 =$ _____

5. $9/14 - 2/21 + 5/7 =$ _____

6. $2/3 + 3/4 - 1/3 =$ _____

7. $1/16 + 3/8 - 1/4 =$ _____

8. $1/5 - 1/15 + 6/25 =$ _____

B. Calculate the value of the following mixed numbers. (1 point each)

1. $6 1/4 - 11 1/12 + 27 2/24 - 9 2/8 =$ _____

2. $56 1/27 - 3 1/18 + 12 1/3 + 4 4/6 =$ _____

3. $3 1/2 + 5 1/3 + 4 3/4 - 2 5/6 =$ _____

4. $1 1/14 - 1/21 + 54 2/3 + 2/7 =$ _____

Score: /12

9/12

Australian Homeschooling #570
Test Your Maths 8

Test 8: Multiplication of Fractions

Calculate the following: (1 point each)

1. $1/2 \times 2/3 =$ _____   2. $5/9 \times 1/11 =$ _____

3. $3/5 \times 3/7 =$ _____   4. $5/12 \times 1/2 =$ _____

5. $2/9 \times 3/10 =$ _____   6. $2 1/2 \times 1/3 =$ _____

7. $7/2 \times 2/5 =$ _____   8. $5 1/2 \times 4 1/2 =$ _____

9. $9/2 \times 5/6 =$ _____   10. $2/7 \times 5 1/4 =$ _____

11. $8 \times 2/8 =$ _____   12. $3/5 \times 9/14 \times 2/3 =$ _____

13. $8/12 \times 12/3 =$ _____   14. $7/8 \times 9/14 \times 1/3 =$ _____

Score: /14

10/14

© Valerie Marett
Coroneos Publications

Australian Homeschooling #570
Test Your Maths 8

Test 9: Division of Fractions

Calculate the following: (1 point each answer)

1. $4/5 \div 1/2 =$ _____

2. $3/2 \div 1/2 =$ _____

3. $10/11 \div 5/11 =$ _____

4. $5/6 \div 10 =$ _____

5. $2/3 \div 4/11 =$ _____

6. $4/5 \div 7/5 =$ _____

7. $2/3 \div 3/7 =$ _____

8. $7/9 \div 11/3 =$ _____

9. $14/5 \div 4/7 =$ _____

10. $7/9 \div 8/12 =$ _____

11. $8 \div 8/3 =$ _____

12. $3/5 \div 2/10 \times 2/3 =$ _____

13. $8/12 \div 16/3 =$ _____

14. $7/6 \times 9/12 \div 1/3 =$ _____

Score: /14

10/14

11

Test 10: Fractions - Fraction Problems

(2 points each answer)

Answer the questions:

1. Joan has $1600. She spends 2/5 of it on a television set and 3/8 on a camera.

   How much does she have left?

   _____

2. After spending 3/4 of his money, John has $80 left.

   How much did John start with?

   _____

3. On a farm there were 84 animals. 2/7 of the animals were pigs and 5/14 were sheep. The rest were horses.

   There were _____ horses on the farm.

4. The farmer had 2500 sheep and goats all together. He bought another 500 sheep. After he bought the sheep the number of sheep equaled the number of goats.

   The farmer had _____ sheep and _____ goats to start with.

5. Bill had 110 yellow and green marbles. He gave 1/3 of the yellow marbles to Janet. He bought another 40 green marbles. He now had equal number of yellow and green marbles.

   To start with Bill had _____ yellow and _____ green marbles.

Score: /14

Pass: 10/14

Australian Homeschooling #570
Test Your Maths 8

Test 11: Percentages of a Number; Fraction to a Percentage; Percentage to a Fraction

(1 point each answer)

A. Answer the following questions.

1. 15% of 200 = _____
2. 12½% of 64 = _____
3. 25% of 64 = _____
4. 20% of 70 = _____
5. 40% of 25 = _____
6. 80% of 250 = _____
7. 5% of 20 = _____
8. 70% of 210= _____
9. 10% of 1,000 = _____
10. 2% of 600 = _____

B. Convert the following fractions to percentages.

1. 1 1/2 = _____
2. 2 1/3 = _____
3. 1/4 = _____
4. 3/5 = _____
5. 4/5 = _____
6. 3/4 = _____
7. 6 1/2 = _____
8. 1/8 = _____
9. 4 3/5 = _____
10. 3/8 = _____

C. Convert the following percentages to a fraction. Simplify the answer.

1. 25% = _____
2. 40% = _____
3. 80% = _____
4. 225% = _____
5. 50% = _____
6. 150% = _____
7. 12.5% = _____
8. 100% = _____
9. 10% = _____
10. 1000% = _____

Score: /30

Pass: 23/30

© Valerie Marett
Coroneos Publications

Australian Homeschooling #570
Test Your Maths 8

Test 12: Percentage Problems

(2 points each answer)

Answer these questions.

1. When Ronald sold his camera for $180 he made a 20% loss on the sale.

   When he bought the camera, he paid $ _____ for it.

   To have made a 20% profit on the sale, he would have had to have

   sold it for $ _____.

2. Simon bought 10 radios at $40 each. He sold 2 at a loss for $30 each.

   He sold the rest for a 20% profit.

   He made a total profit on the sale of $ _____.

3. Cindy had $160. She spent 75% of her money on shoes and the rest

   on dresses. The dresses were $10 each.

   She bought _____ dresses.

4. After selling 80% of his apples, the greengrocer had 13 left.

   How many apples did the greengrocer have to start with?

   _____ apples.

5. The farmer bought 60 ducks for $4 dollars each.

   He sold them for $312.

   He made $ _____ profit.

   He marked up the price of the ducks by _____ %.

6. Sam bought a toy car for $2 and sold it for $3.78.

   What percentage of the buying price did he sell it for?

   _____ %

7. Albert weighs 20 kg. His father weighs 300% more than Albert.

   Albert's father weighs _____ kg.

8. Jill bought a box for $3.50. She then spent $1.50 to paint it

   Jill sold the box for $8.00.

   Her percentage profit was _____ %.

Score: _____ /20

Pass: 16/20

© Valerie Marett
Coroneos Publications

Australian Homeschooling #570
Test Your Maths 8

Test 13: More Percentage Problems

(1 point each answer)

Answer these questions.

1. Sam bought 15 chairs for $20 each. He sold 5 for $30 each.

   He sold the rest for a 25% profit.

   Sam made a profit of $_____

   He made a profit of _____% on his purchase price.

2. Calculate the interest on 13,000 for 9 months at the interest rate of

   8% per annum.

   $ _____

3. Penny has $240. She spent 40% on books and the rest buying 6 skirts

   for which she paid $24 each.

   She bought _____ skirts.

4. Peter and John's savings are in the ratio of 7 : 3.

   When Peter's savings decreased by 50%, their total savings were $140

   (a) Peter started with $ _____

   (b) Peter now has $ _____

   (c) John started with $ _____

   (d) John now has $ _____

5. Jenny spent 60% of her money on entertainment and half the

   remainder on a book. She had $10 left.

   How much money did she have to start with? $ _____

6. There are 48 socks in a draw.

   25% of the socks are red.   33% of the socks are black.

   16.6% of the socks are white.   The rest of the socks are brown.

   (a) _____% of the socks are brown.

   (b) There are _____ red socks.   **(c)** There are _____ black socks.

   (d) There are _____ white socks.   **(e)** There are _____ brown socks.

Score: /14   **Pass: 11/14**

© Valerie Marett
Coroneos Publications

Australian Homeschooling #570
Test Your Maths 8

Test 14: Decimals

(1 point each answer)

A. Write the decimal number for each of the following.

1. 3 ones 5 tenths = _____

2. Four ones six thousandths = _____

3. 6 hundreds 4 tens 2 tenths = _____

4. 2 thousand 5 hundred 2 tenths 8 hundredths = _____

5. 2 ones 6 tenths 3 hundredths 2 thousandths = _____

B. Find the value of the following.

1. 6.973 + 0.34 = _____   2. 748.001 + 3.73 = _____

3. 8.9 + 0.00467 = _____   4. 268 + 0.00426 = _____

5. Add 5 tenths to 7 thousandths = _____

6. Add 5 tens 8 ones 3 tenths to 47.058 = _____

7. Subtract 7 hundredths and 4 tenths from 0.999 = _____

8. Multiply 6 by 3 tenths = _____

9. Multiply 0.5 by 0.3 = _____

10. Multiply 8.4 by 0.5 = _____

Score: ____ /15

Pass: 12/15

Australian Homeschooling #570
Test Your Maths 8

Test 15: Adding and Subtracting Decimals

A. Fill in the blanks. (1 point each question)

1. $1.5 + 2.3 =$ _____

2. $0.76 + 2 =$ _____

3. $7.6 - 1.7 =$ _____

4. $5 - 2.4 =$ _____

5. $1.06 + 0.88 =$ _____

6. $3.28 - 0.12 =$ _____

7. $5.76 - 2.98 =$ _____

8. $1.88 + 9.68 =$ _____

B. Complete the following: (1 point)

1.
```
  0.66
+ 0.08
_____
```

2.
```
  0.03
+ 0.58
_____
```

3.
```
  8.57
- 5.38
_____
```

4.
```
 10.68
- 4.94
_____
```

5.
```
 46.87
+18.16
_____
```

6.
```
 15.74
- 7.38
_____
```

C. Fill in the missing numbers. (1 point each space)

1.
```
  80.7_
- 15.68
_____
  65.02
```

2.
```
 76.84
+1_.09
_____
 91.93
```

3.
```
 1_.76
+56.88
_____
 74.64
```

4.
```
 _8.34
-29.65
_____
 18.69
```

Score: /18

Pass: 14 /18

Australian Homeschooling #570
Test Your Maths 8

Test 16: Word Problems—Addition & Subtraction of Decimals

Answer the following word problems. (2 points each question)

1. John had $37.42. His mother gave him $5.75 for cleaning the windows and his father gave him a further $10. 99. How much money does John have in total?

   _____

2. I have collected 23.67 kg of cans for recycling. My sister, Elizabeth, has collected 3.75 kg more than I have. What is the total weight of the recycled cans we have to take for recycling?

   _____

3. I left home with $56.00. I spent $2.30 on bus fares; $1.55 on a drink; $27.33 at the supermarket and $9.95 at the greengrocers. How much money do I have left?

   _____

4. Joel weighs 27.5 kg, Krystal weighs 23.24 kg, Olivia weighs 22.55 and Madeline weighs 19.76 kg. What is the total weight of my four grandchildren?

   _____

5. Mum had a 25kg bag of flour. She used 12.25 kg to make 6 loaves of bread and 55g to make a sauce for dinner. How much flour has she left?

   _____

6. Peter drank 2.4 litres of cold water, Frankie drank 1.75 litres and Joel drank 3.24 litres. If Mum had 10 litres of water in the refrigerator, how many litres of water were left?

   _____

Score: /12   **Pass: 9 /12**

© Valerie Marett
Coroneos Publications

Australian Homeschooling #570
Test Your Maths 8

Test 17: More Decimals
(1 point each answer)

A. Answer the questions.

1. 0.22 x 500 = _____

2. 8.24 x 400 = _____

3. 18.2 x 8000 = _____

4. 0.001 x 0.02 = _____

5. 0.23 x 0.2 = _____

6. 18.2 x 1000 = _____

7. 7.2 ÷ 200 = _____

8. 689 ÷ 6.89 = _____

B. Find the equivalent measures.

1. 0.5 kg = _____gm

2. 450 g = _____kg

3. 0.4 L = _____ml

4. 2357 m = _____km

5. 0.25 cm = _____mm

6. $649 = _____cents

7. 45.589 m = _____mm

8. 54.72 cm = _____mm

C. Round to two decimal places.

1. 7.4892 _____

2. 0.0372 _____

3. 2,020 _____

4. 935.22 _____

5. 63.75294 _____

6. 2,548,502.682 _____

7. 0.175 _____

8. 85.299 _____

Score: /24   **Pass: 16/24**

Test 18: Multiplication of Decimals

A. Find the value of the following: (1 point each)

1. $0.8 x 5 = _____

2. $0.04 x 3 = _____

3. $6 x 0.75 = _____

4. $0.9 x 6 = _____

5. $1.35 x 8 = _____

6. $ 7.35 x 7 = _____

7. 9 x 1.54 = _____

8. 12.7 x 6 = _____

9. 43.2 x 7 = _____

10. 1.33 x 5 = _____

11. 12.85 x 4 = _____

12. 55.78 x 8 = _____

B. Multiply the following: (1 point each)

1. 5 tenths x 2 = _____

2. 6 hundredths x 4 = _____

3. 2 ones 4 tenths 5 hundredths x 9 = _____

4. 23 ones 2 tenths and 2 hundredths x 6 = _____

5. 10 ones 11 hundredths x 7 = _____

6. 7 ones 67 hundredths x 3 = _____

7. 77 ones 6 tenths 4 hundredths x 5 = _____

8. 3 ones 9 tenths x 3 = _____

9. 44 ones 1 hundredth x 7 = _____

10. 24 ones 6 tenths 3 hundredths x 5 = _____

11. 4 tenths 0 hundredths x 8 = _____

12. Six ones two tenths five hundredths x 3 = _____

Score: /24

Pass: 18 /24

© Valerie Marett
Coroneos Publications

20

Test 19: Division of Decimals

Find the value of the following in decimals: (1 point each)

1. $15 \div 4 =$ _____

2. $2.36 \div 4 =$ _____

3. $5.28 \div 3 =$ _____

4. $8.52 \div 6 =$ _____

5. $9.6 \div 4 =$ _____

6. $0.12 \div 3 =$ _____

7. $7.65 \div 9 =$ _____

8. $4.72 \div 8 =$ _____

9. $4.97 \div 7 =$ _____

10. $7.218 \div 9 =$ _____

11. $6 \div 8 =$ _____

12. $14.55 \div 5 =$ _____

13. $2.01 \div 3 =$ _____

Score: /13   **Pass: 10 /13**

© Valerie Marett
Coroneos Publications

Australian Homeschooling #570
Test Your Maths 8

Test 20: Word Problems - Multiplication and Division of Decimals

Answer the following problems: (4 points question 6, 2 points remaining problems)

1. John bought a 20kg bag of flour. He divided the flour equally into 8 bags. How much flour was in each bag?

   _____

2. Joel bought 6 hamburgers that each cost $2.75 and 6 large fries each costing $1.50. How much change would he have from $100?

   _____

3. Peter sold $50 worth of lollies. He sold 30 bags of lollies at $0.75. He sold the rest at $0.50. How many bags of lollies did he sell at $0.50?

   _____

4. If I divide 8 litres of soft drink among 10 children, how many litres of soft drink will each child receive?

   _____

5. Krystal had 6 presents for her friends. The largest present weighed 2.2 kg and the smallest present weighed 0.8 kg. The total weight of the presents was 9.4 kg. What was the average weight of each of the other 4 parcels?

   _____

6. At the shops I bought 6 packets of pasta at $1.25 each; 3 litres of milk at $2.10 per litre; 1.5 kg of tomatoes at $3 per kilogram and 2 bottles of soft drink at $1.95 per bottle. What was the total cost of my shopping? How much money would I need to have in my purse in total if I had to pay an electricity bill of $142.75 on the way home?

   _____   _____

Score: ___/14

Pass: 10 /14

Australian Homeschooling #570
Test Your Maths 8

Test 21: Converting Decimals to Fractions
Converting Fractions to Decimals

A. Convert the decimal number to a fraction. (1 point each answer)

1. 3.25 = _____   **2.** 0.875 = _____

3. 47.8 = _____   **4.** 0.01 = _____

5. 17.75 = _____   **6.** 10.2 = _____

7. 49.6 = _____   **8.** 30.35 = _____

9. 573.085 = _____   **10.** 47.7 = _____

11. 0.0036 = _____   **12.** 9,587.124 = _____

B. Convert the fraction to a decimal number (1 point each answer)

1. 89 7/25 = _____   **2.** 4 3/8 = _____

3. 2,398 5/100 = _____   **4.** 32/64 = _____

5. 2 3/4 = _____   **6.** 7/8 = _____

7. 37 3/4 = _____   **8.** 7,024 5/15 = _____

9. 857 9/18 = _____   **10.** 64/256 = _____

11. 200,347 91/12 = _____   **12.** 347,469 3/8= _____

Score: /24

20/24

© Valerie Marett
Coroneos Publications

Australian Homeschooling #570
Test Your Maths 8

Test 22: Rounding Decimals
Converting Decimals to Percentages
Converting Percentages to Decimals
Converting Fractions to Percentages

A. Round the number to two decimal places   (1 point each answer)

1. 76.9723   = _____   2. 0.274   = _____

3. 0.260   = _____   4. 0.082   = _____

5. 4,892.538   = _____   6. 11.1118   = _____

7. 87.677   = _____   8. 4.0003   = _____

B. Convert the decimal number to a percentage   (1 point each answer)

1. 0.50   = _____   2. 1.37   = _____

3. 2.865   = _____   4. 16.90   = _____

5. 0.05   = _____   6. 10.2   = _____

7. 0.0496   = _____   8. .3035   = _____

C. Convert the fraction to a percentage   (1 point each answer)

1. 1/3   = _____   2. 3/4   = _____

3. 2 1/2   = _____   4. 7/8   = _____

5. 3 1/20   = _____   6. 13/50   = _____

7. 7/25   = _____   8. 3 9/25   = _____

Score: /24   **20/24**

© Valerie Marett
Coroneos Publications

Australian Homeschooling #570
Test Your Maths 8

Test 23: Converting Fractions to Percentages
Multiplication of Decimals
Division of Decimals

A. Multiply the following.   (1 point each answer)

1. 24.56 x 11   = _____

2. 12 x 12.5   = _____

3. 0.4 x 3   = _____

4. 2.4 x 10   = _____

5. 4,100 x 0.2   = _____

6. 0.5 x 0.5   = _____

7. 0.16 x 0.05   = _____

8. 13.46 x 0.25   = _____

9. 46 X 0.50   = _____

10. 38 X 0.24   = _____

11. 1.2 X 3   = _____

12. 0.18 X 60   = _____

13. 0.05 X 5   = _____

14. 1.32 X 110   = _____

15. 10.00 X 1,000.00 = _____

16. 100 X 10,000 = _____

B. Divide the following. Give your answer in decimals.   (1 point each answer)

1.   56 ÷ 0.10 =   _____

2. 32 ÷ 0.05 =   _____

3. 0.10 ÷ 5 =   _____

4. 2.3 ÷ 4.6 =   _____

5. 7.2 ÷ 0.9 =   _____

6. 1.44 ÷ 1.2 =   _____

7. 8.4 ÷ 7 =   _____

8. 1.0 ÷ 100 =   _____

9. 3469 ÷ 0.5 =   _____

10. 0.17598 ÷ 0.07 = _____

11. 0.8448 ÷ 0.8 =   _____

12. 763.896 ÷ 0.08 = _____

13. 4.7124 ÷ 0.9 =   _____

14. 359.19 ÷ 0.04 = _____

Score: /30   **20/30**

Test 24: Factors and Multiples

(1 point each answer)

A. Write down the prime factors of the following numbers.

1. 18 _____

2. 12 _____

3. 150 _____

4. 96 _____

5. 144 _____

6. 225 _____

7. 126 _____

8. 999 _____

B. Write the answer.

1. 12 x 6 + 6 + 6 + 6 + 6 = 6 x _____

2. 9 x 6 x 1 x 2 = 3 x 2 x _____

3. 16 x 21 x 2 = 32 x 7 x _____

4. 63 x 2 = 3 x _____

C. Write the answer.

1. The second largest prime factor of 210 is _____

2. The sum of the smallest and biggest prime factor of 13 _____

3. Which numbers are a factor of 72?

   1, 2, 3, 5, 7, 11 _____

4. List all the prime factors of 200 _____

5. Which of the following numbers have 16 as a factor?

   32, 36, 128, 248, 796, 1024 _____

6. Which numbers are factors of 63?

   1, 2, 3, 4, 5, 9, 21, 27, 36, 63 _____

7. Find the sum of all of the prime factors of 24 _____

8. The largest prime factor of 132 is _____

Score: /20

Pass: 16/20

© Valerie Marett
Coroneos Publications

Australian Homeschooling #570
Test Your Maths 8

Test 25: Highest Common Factor (HCF)
(1 point each answer)

A. Find all the common factors of:

1. 48 and 72 _____

2. 220 and 44 _____

3. 56 and 14 _____

4. 27 and 36 _____

B. Find the highest common factor of:

1. 6 and 12 _____ **2.** 36 and 18 _____

3. 20 and 14 _____ **4.** 16 and 96 _____

5. 27 and 63 _____ **6.** 15 and 90 _____

7. 144 and 48 _____ **8.** 56 and 112 _____

Lowest Common Multiple (LCM)
(1 point each answer)

A. Find the lowest common multiple for each of the following pairs of numbers

1. 13 and 26 _____ **2.** 8 and 9 _____

3. 36 and 27 _____ **4.** 4 and 12 _____

5. 15 and 50 _____ **6.** 8 and 28 _____

7. 2 and 5 _____ **8.** 3 and 10 _____

B. Find the HCF and LCM for the following pairs of numbers

	HCF	LCM
1. 8 and 24	_____	_____
2. 24 and 9	_____	_____
3. 16 and 128	_____	_____

Score: /26

Pass: 20/26

Test 26: Index Notation

A. Factorize the numbers into prime numbers using index notation where possible

1. 96 _____

2. 256 _____

3. 315 _____

4. 216 _____

5. 2,200 _____

6. 10,000,000 _____

B. Find the value of:

1. $2^2 \times 3 + 4 =$ _____

2. $4 \times 5^2 =$ _____

3. $3 \times (4 + 5) \times 3^2 =$ _____

4. $81 \div 3^3 + 69 + 7^2 =$ _____

5. $2^2 + 3^2 + 2^3 =$ _____

6. $(8 - 2^3) \times 16 =$ _____

C. Write the following in index notation using prime numbers

1. three squared _____

2. seven cubed _____

3. twenty seven _____

4. eight _____

4. forty-nine _____

6. five squared _____

D. Answer these questions using index notation

1. $2 \times 2 \times 2 \times 2 \times 2 + 16 =$ _____

2. $3^2 + 3^2 + 3^2 =$ _____

3. $3 \times 3 \times 3 \times 3 \times 7 \times 7 \times 7 =$ _____

4. $81 \div 3 \div 3 \div 3 =$ _____

5. $1,000,000 + 5,000,000 =$ _____

6. $32 - 16 =$ _____

7. $27 \div 9 =$ _____

8. $256 \div 4 \div 4 \div 2 =$ _____

Score: /26

Pass: 18/26

Test 27: Ratios
(1 point each question)

Express each of the following ratios in its simplest form:

1. 18 : 12 = _____ : _____

2. 16 : 24 = _____ : _____

3. 20 : 25 = _____ : _____

4. 60 : 120 = _____ : _____

5. 49 : 14 = _____ : _____

6. 27 : 9 = _____ : _____

Answer the questions.
(1 point each question)

Tom is three years old.
John is five years old.
Peter is ten years old.

1. The ratio of Tom's age to Peter's age is _____ : _____

2. The ratio of John's age to the total of their ages is

   _____ : _____

3. The ratio of Peter's age to the total of their ages is

   _____ : _____

4. The ratio of John's age to the Tom's age is _____ : _____

5. Joan and Ann weigh a total of 60kg.

   The ratio of Joan's weight to Ann's weight is 2 : 1.

   Ann weighs _____kg.

Sam is four times as old as Jack.
Jack is two years old.

6. What is the ratio of Sam's age to Jack's age? _____ : _____

7. What is the ratio of Jack's age to Sam's age? _____ : _____

8. How old is Sam? _____

9. What is the age difference between Sam and Jack? _____

Score: /15

Pass: 12/15

© Valerie Marett
Coroneos Publications

Australian Homeschooling #570
Test Your Maths 8

Test 28: Relationship between Ratios and Fractions
(1 point each answer)
Answer the questions.

1. There are 64 socks in the drawer. The ratio of blue, green and red socks in a draw is 3 : 6 : 7.

   (a) What fraction of the socks are blue? _____

   (b) What fraction of the socks are green? _____

   (c) What fraction of the socks are red? _____

   (d) There are _____ blue socks in the draw.

   (e) There are _____ green socks in the draw.

   (f) There are _____ red socks in the draw.

2. Anne, Elizabeth and Jill were paid their pocket money. Elizabeth received 1/7 of the money. The remainder was divided between Anne and Jill in the ratio of 2 : 4. If Elizabeth received $10 then Anne received $_____.

3. 5/8 of the fruit in the bowl are apples. If there are fifteen apples in the bowl. How many pieces other pieces of fruit are there in the bowl? _____

4. 3/4 of the people at the party were children. The remainder of the people were men and woman in the ratio of 2 : 3. At the party there were 8 men _____ women and _____ children.

5. Jack, Bill and Ben have 39 toys which they own in the ratio of 4 : 7 : 2.

   (a) Jack owns _____ toys.

   (b) Bill owns _____ toys.

   (c) Ben owns _____ toys.

6. The ratio of Amy's age to Beth's age is 7 : 4. Amy is now 28 years old.

   (a) Beth is _____ years old.

   (b) Their total age is _____ years.

   (c) In ten years their total age will be _____ years.

   (d) Amy was _____ years old when Beth was born.

Score: ___/17

Pass: 13/17

Australian Homeschooling #570
Test Your Maths 8

Test 29: Perimeter

(1 point each answer)

Find the perimeters of the following shapes. (1 point each answer)

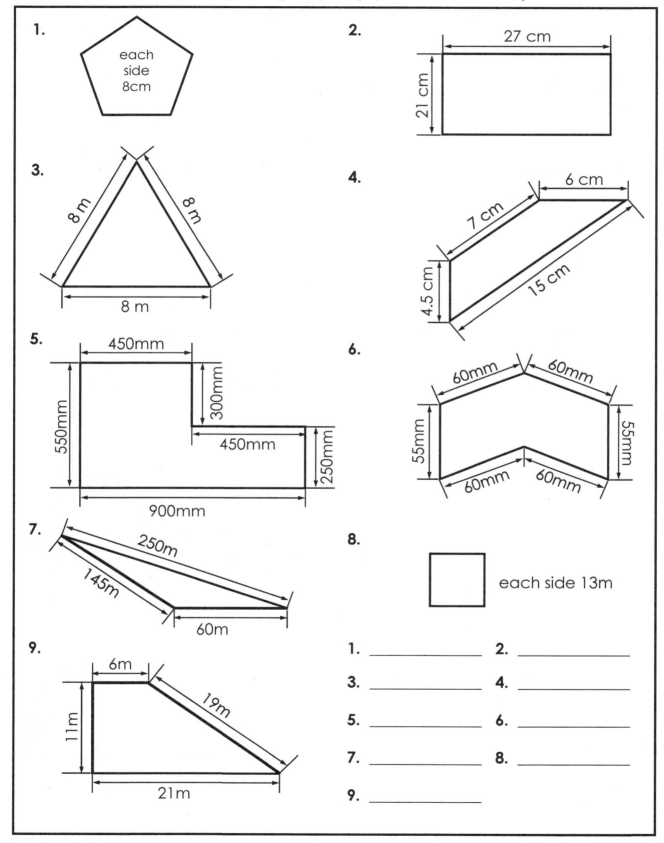

1.

each side 8cm

2.

27 cm

21 cm

3.

8 m

8 m

8 m

4.

6 cm

7 cm

15 cm

4.5 cm

5.

450mm

300mm

550mm

450mm

250mm

900mm

6.

60mm 60mm

55mm 55mm

60mm 60mm

7.

250m

145m

60m

8.

each side 13m

9.

6m

19m

11m

21m

1. _____ 2. _____

3. _____ 4. _____

5. _____ 6. _____

7. _____ 8. _____

9. _____

Score: /9

7/9

© Valerie Marett
Coroneos Publications

Australian Homeschooling #570
Test Your Maths 8

Test 30: Area of a Triangle

Calculate the area of each triangle in square centimetres.
(1 point each question.)

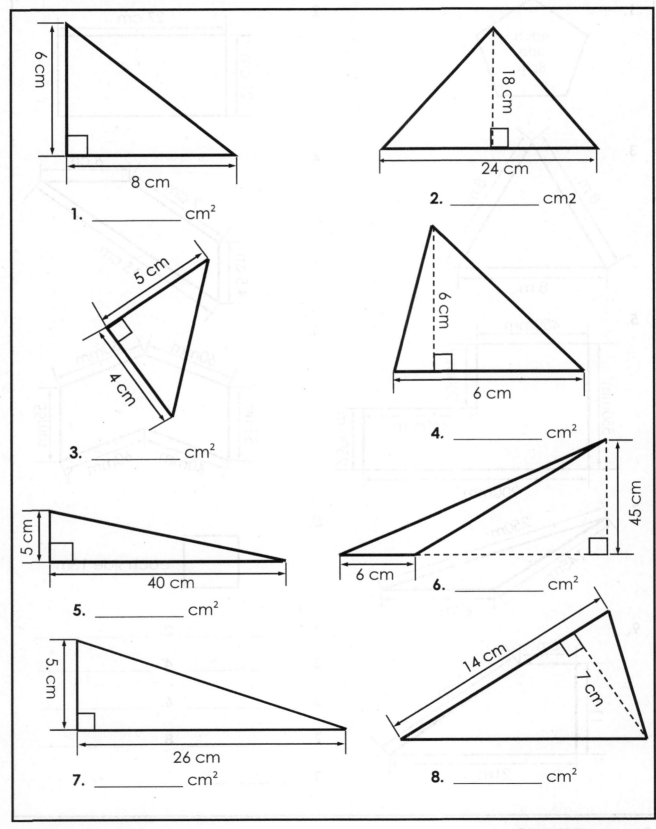

1. _____ cm²

2. _____ cm2

3. _____ cm²

4. _____ cm²

5. _____ cm²

6. _____ cm²

7. _____ cm²

8. _____ cm²

Australian Homeschooling #570
Test Your Maths 8

Test 31: Area of Composite Figures

(1 point each answer)

Calculate the area of the following shapes. (1 point each answer)

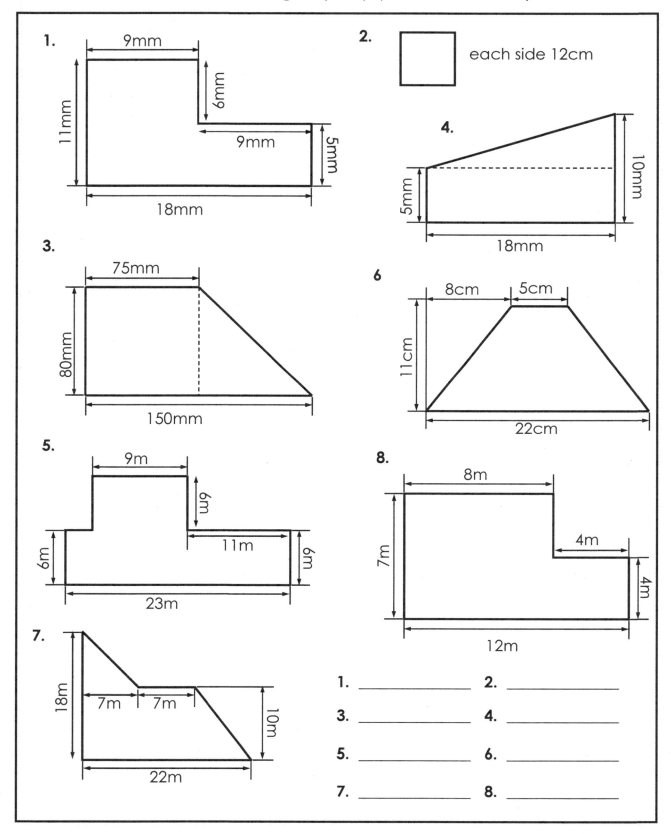

1. _____   2. _____

3. _____   4. _____

5. _____   6. _____

7. _____   8. _____

Test 32: Volume

Answer the questions (2 points each question)

1. 200 identical marbles are removed from a rectangular tank full of water. The water level dropped by two thirds after the marbles were removed. The tank measures 60cm x 100cm x 20cm. What is the volume of one marble in millilitres?

   Volume = _____ ml.

2. A rectangular tank measures 6cm x 9cm 20 cm. The tank is one third full of water . How much water is required to fill the tank to the brim?

   Quantity of water = _____ ml.

3. The base of a rectangular tank measures 50mm x 40 mm. If 200ml of water is poured into the tank how much will the level rise?

   The water level increases _____ mm.

4. A rectangular tank contains 4 litres of water. The base of the tank measures 40cm x 100 cm. What is the height of the water in the tank?

   Height of water = _____ mm.

© Valerie Marett
Coroneos Publications

Australian Homeschooling #570
Test Your Maths 8

33: Volume - Calculating Length, Breadth and Height

Given the volume calculate the length, breadth and height
(2 points each answer)

1. Volume = 27m³

   h = _____ m

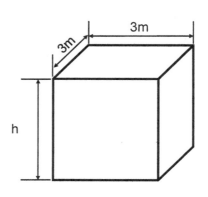

2. Volume = 5760m³

   h = _____ m

3. The volume = 840m³

   l = _____ m

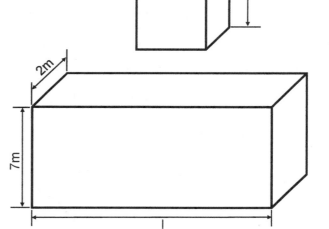

4. The volume = 240m³

   h = _____ m

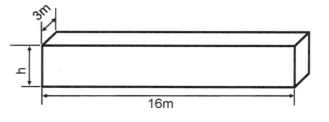

Australian Homeschooling #570
Test Your Maths 8

Test 34 : Circles - Circumference
(2 points each answer)

Answer these questions.

1. The radius of a circle is 20 mm. (Use 3.14 for the value of π)

   The circumference of the circle is _____ mm

2. The diameter of a circle is 3 metres. (Use 3.14 for the value of π)

   The circumference of the circle is _____ m.

3. The circumference of a circle is 66 metres. (Use 3 1/7 for the value of π)

   (a) The diameter of the circle is _____ metres.

   (b) The radius of the circle is _____ metres.

4. The circle touches the sides of the square on all four sides.

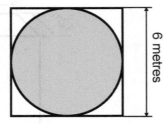

6 metres

(Use 3.14 for the value of π)

   (a) The radius of the circle is _____ m.

   (b) The diameter of the circle is _____ m.

   (c) The circumference of the circle is _____ m.

5. Calculate the perimeter of the semi-circle.

   (Use 3 1/7 for the value of π)

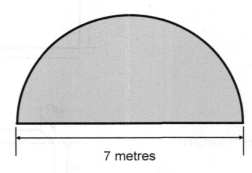

7 metres

   The perimeter of the semicircle is _____

Score: /16

Pass: 12/16

Australian Homeschooling #570
Test Your Maths 8

Test 35: Circles - Area
(2 points each answer)

Answer these questions.

1. The radius of a circle is 7 cm. (Use 3 1/7 for the value of π)

   The area of the circle is _____ cm².

2. The diameter of a circle is 40 mm. (Use 3.14 for the value of π)

   The area of the circle is _____ cm².

3. The square has a perimeter of 40 metres.
   Inside the square there are four circles of
   Similar size. The circles touch each other
   and the sides of the square.
   (Use 3.14 for the value of π)

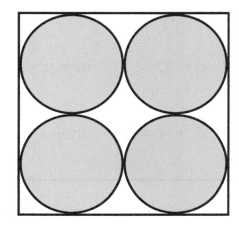

   (a) The total area of the 4 circles = _____ m².

   (b) The area of the unshaded area = _____ m².

   (c) The circumference of one of the circles is _____ m.

4. The large circle is one metre in diameter.
   The small circle is half the diameter of the
   large circle.
   Calculate the area of the shaded part in
   terms of n.

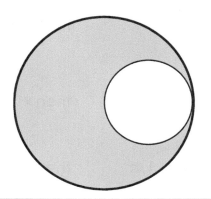

   Area = _____ nm².

Score: /12

Pass: 6/12

© Valerie Marett
Coroneos Publications

Australian Homeschooling #570
Test Your Maths 8

Test 36: Algebra—Finding a Value

A. Find the value of x. (1 point each)

1. $x^2 = 16$ then x = _____
2. $4x = 24x$ then x = _____

3. $x = 3 + 5$ then x = _____
4. $2x = 17 - 5$ then x = _____

5. $6x + 24 = 48$ then x = _____
6. $x/2 = 100$ then x = _____

7. $x^3 = 27$ then x = _____
8. $3x - 20 = 16$ then x = _____

9. $x^2 + 4 = 20$ then x = _____
10. $5x = 3x5$ then x = _____

B. Find the value of x, given that a =4, b = 2 , c=6. (1 point each)

1. $x = a + b + c$ then x = _____
2. $4x = a$ then x = _____

3. $x = c + 5$ then x = _____
4. $x^2 = a$ then x = _____

5. $3x = c$ then x = _____
6. $x/a = 100$ then x = _____

7. $x = abc$ then x = _____
8. $x + 2b = 24$ then x = _____

9. $1/x = 1/c$ then x = _____
10. $c/x = 2$ then x = _____

Score: /20

16/20

© Valerie Marett
Coroneos Publications

Australian Homeschooling #570
Test Your Maths 8

Test 37 : Algebraic Substitution
(1 point each answer)

A. Find the value of each expression given that a = 9, b = 2 and c = 3.

1. $8ab - 3c =$ _____

2. $2ab - 3a + 4c =$ _____

3. $ab^2 - c =$ _____

4. $4a - b + 5c =$ _____

5. $3ab + 4c =$ _____

6. $7(4a - c) + 56 =$ _____

B. Find the value of each expression.

1. If $m = 7$, $n = 0$ and $p = 3$, then $8mp - 10mn =$ _____

2. If $x = 10$ and $y = 5$, then $(x^2 - 5) \div y =$ _____

3. If $x = 3$ and $y = 4$, then $x^2 + y^2 =$ _____

4. If $d = 0$ and $f = 7$, then $4df^2 + 34 =$ _____

5. If $a = 6$ and $b = 2$, then $4ab - b =$ _____

6. If $g = 8$ and $k = 1$, then $7g + 25k - 9gk =$ _____

7. If $x = 5$ and $y = 2$, then $5y^2 + 4x^2 =$ _____

8. $a = 6$ and $b = 10$, then $(b - a)(b + a) =$ _____

9. $h = -4$ and $t = 1$, then $3t(8t - 5h) =$ _____

10. If $x = 16$ and $y = 12$, then $\frac{1}{8}$ of $3xy =$ _____

Score: /16   **Pass: 12/16**

Test 38: Algebraic Simplification

(1 point each answer)

A. Expand and simplify.

1. $2(2a + 3) + 3(3a + 5)$ = _____

2. $4(2x + 1) + 2(x + 2)$ = _____

3. $6(2s + 3) - 2(5s + 8)$ = _____

4. $a(a + b) + a(2a + 5b)$ = _____

5. $2h(h + t) + h(t - 2h)$ = _____

6. $7(a + 3b) + (2a - 4b)$ = _____

7. $-5(b - c) - 3(c - b)$ = _____

8. $-3(p - q) - (2p - 3q)$ = _____

9. $8(x - y - 3) + 2(2x + y + 3)$ = _____

10. $5(6 + 2p - 3q) - 2(1 - 3p + q)$ = _____

Score: ___/10

Pass: 7/10

© Valerie Marett
Coroneos Publications

Australian Homeschooling #570
Test Your Maths 8

Test 39: Algebraic Simplification 2

(2 points each answer)

A. Simplify.

1. $\dfrac{8ab}{4a}$ = _____

2. $\dfrac{7}{21d}$ = _____

3. $\dfrac{7yz}{21z}$ = _____

4. $\dfrac{6p^2}{3p}$ = _____

5. $\dfrac{2a^2b}{2ab}$ = _____

6. $\dfrac{3p^2q^2}{4pq}$ = _____

7. $\dfrac{9s}{10} + \dfrac{2s}{15} + \dfrac{s}{5}$ = _____

8. $\dfrac{x+3}{5} + \dfrac{x+4}{10}$ = _____

Score: /16

Pass: 12/16

© Valerie Marett
Coroneos Publications

Australian Homeschooling #570
Test Your Maths 8

Test 40: Algebraic Simplification 3
(2 points each answer)

A. Simplify.

1. $\dfrac{a^2b}{bc} \times \dfrac{c}{a}$ = _____

2. $\dfrac{2st}{sq} \times \dfrac{qr}{4r^2}$ = _____

3. $\dfrac{p^2q}{r} \div \dfrac{pq}{r}$ = _____

4. $\dfrac{y^2z}{z} \div \dfrac{yz}{z}$ = _____

5. $\dfrac{4ab}{5c} \times \dfrac{15c}{2a} \times \dfrac{7a}{3b}$ = _____

6. $\dfrac{2ab}{3c} \times \dfrac{9cd}{4b} \div \dfrac{6a}{7}$ = _____

7. $\dfrac{4mn}{5p} \times \dfrac{15pq}{4mr} \div \dfrac{3q}{r}$ = _____

8. $\dfrac{9ph}{h^2} \times \dfrac{10k}{3p} \div \dfrac{5k}{ph}$ = _____

Score: /16

Pass: 12/16

© Valerie Marett
Coroneos Publications

Australian Homeschooling #570
Test Your Maths 8

Test 41: Algebra: Expand Brackets

(2 points each answer)

Expand and simplify.

1. $(a^3 b^2)^4$ = _____

2. $(2a^3 b^2)^2$ = _____

3. $(12a^2 b^3)^3$ = _____

4. $(5a^2 b^3 c^4)^2$ = _____

5. $\left\{ \dfrac{a^2}{b^3} \right\}^2$ = _____

6. $\left\{ \dfrac{2a^4}{bc^2} \right\}^3$ = _____

7. $\left\{ \dfrac{6a^2b}{2c^4} \right\}^2$ = _____

Score: /14

Pass: 10/14

© Valerie Marett
Coroneos Publications

Australian Homeschooling #570
Test Your Maths 8

Test 42: Geometry

Answer the questions. (2 points each question)

1.

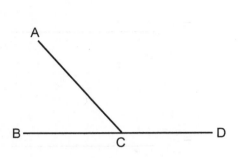

∡ACB = 45°

∡ACD = _____°

2.

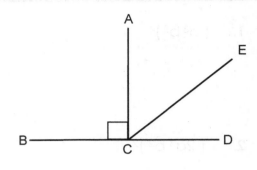

∡ECD = 45°

∡ACE = _____°

3.

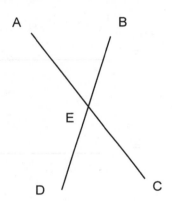

∡AEB = 40°

∡DEC = _____°

4.

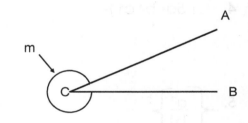

∡ACB = 30°

∡m = _____°

5. BCD is a straight line

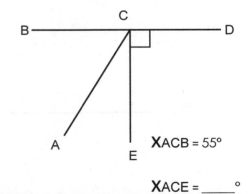

∡ACB = 55°

∡ACE = _____°

6.

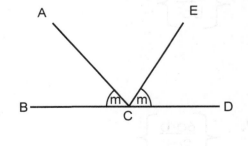

∡m = 30°

∡ACE = _____°

Score: /12   **Pass: 9/12**

Australian Homeschooling #570
Test Your Maths 8

Test 43 : Triangles and Parallelograms

(2 points each question)

Find the unknown angles in the following figures. (Not drawn to scale.)

1.

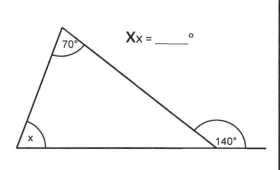

X x = _____ °

2.

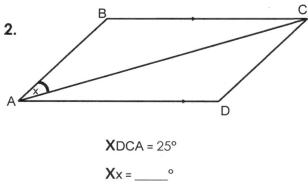

X DCA = 25°

X x = _____ °

3.

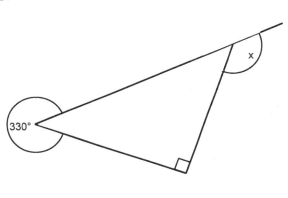

X x = _____ °

4.

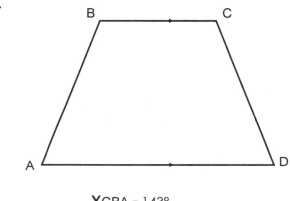

X CBA = 143°

X BAD = _____ °

5.

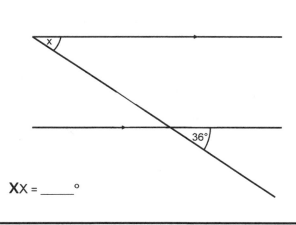

X X = _____ °

6.

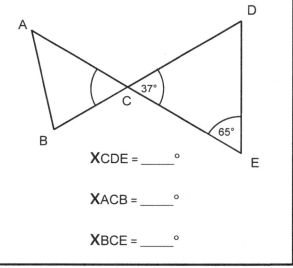

X CDE = _____ °

X ACB = _____ °

X BCE = _____ °

Score: /12   **Pass: 9/12**

© Valerie Marett
Coroneos Publications

Australian Homeschooling #570
Test Your Maths 8

Test 44: Triangles and Parallelograms
(2 points each question.)
Find the unknown angles in the following figures. (Not drawn to scale.)

1.

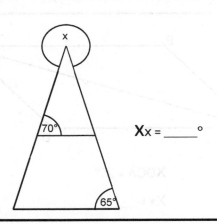

$Xx =$ _____ °

2.

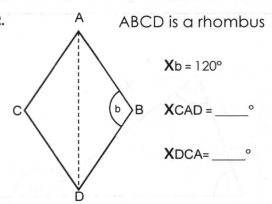

ABCD is a rhombus

$Xb = 120°$

$XCAD =$ _____ °

$XDCA =$ _____ °

3.

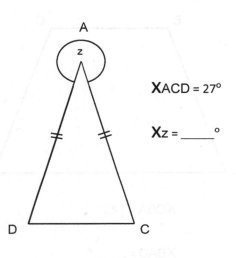

$XACD = 27°$

$Xz =$ _____ °

4.

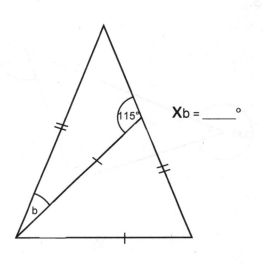

$Xb =$ _____ °

5. ABCD is a rectangle

$Xs =$ _____ °

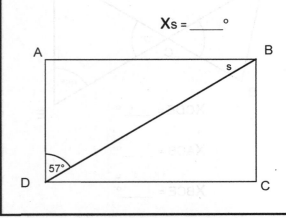

6.

ABCD is a parallelogram

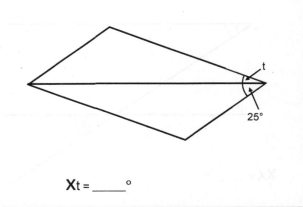

$Xt =$ _____ °

© Valerie Marett
Coroneos Publications

Australian Homeschooling #570
Test Your Maths 8

Test 45: Bar Graphs

A. On a separate sheet of paper draw a bar graph to compare the population of the Capital cities of Australia in 2015. The amount of people in each city is shown below.
(10 points)

Sydney:	4,526,470
Melbourne:	4,353,515
Brisbane:	2,209,450
Perth	1,958,916
Adelaide	1,288,682
Canberra	424,666
Hobart	209,254
Darwin	123,396

B. Look the bar graph below. It shows the temperature in Australia's capital cities on a September day. Answer the questions below based on this graph.
(1 point each space)

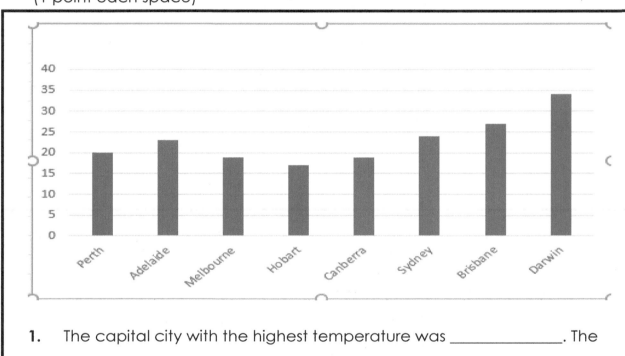

1. The capital city with the highest temperature was _____. The temperature was _____.

2. The capital city with the lowest temperature was _____. The temperature was _____.

3. _____ and _____ had the same temperature.

4. In _____ cities the temperature was over 20°C

5. Which coast was hotter? The east or the west coast? _____

Score: /18   **Pass: 13/18**

Australian Homeschooling #570
Test Your Maths 8

Test 46: Pie Graphs

A. On a separate sheet of paper draw a pie graph to compare the amount of people who owned pets in Australia. The number of each pet kept is shown below. (10 points)

2.34 million owned cats
3.75 million owned dogs
20 million owned fish
9 million owned birds
3 million owned other pets, e.g., horses, goats etc.

B. Look the pie graph below. It shows the sports played by children between 6 and 16. Answer the questions below based on this graph.
(1 point each space)

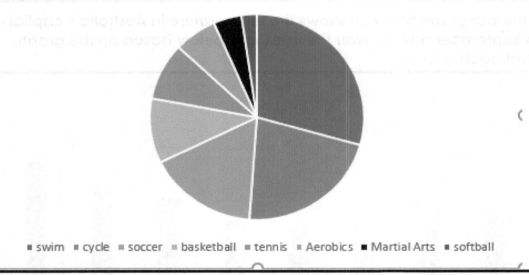

■ swim ■ cycle ■ soccer ■ basketball ■ tennis ■ Aerobics ■ Martial Arts ■ softball

1. The most popular sport was _____. The least popular sport was

_____.

2. The third most popular sport was _____.

3. The total number of children surveyed were 10,731. If 16% played

soccer, how many children played? _____

4. 2,342 children cycled and 457 learnt martial arts. What was the total

percentage of children who played these games? _____

5. The three least popular activities attracted only 1402 children. What were

these sports? _____ , _____, _____. What

percentage of the total number of children were they? _____

48

Test 47: Cartesian Planes

A. Complete the table of values for the following equations and list the co-ordinate pairs. (1 point each blank)

y = 3x

x	-2	-1	0	1	2
y					
(x, y					

B. Construct a set of axes so that x axes goes (by .5) from –2.5 to 2.5 and the y axis (by 1's) from –8 to 8. (5 points)

C. Complete the table of values for the following equations and list the co-ordinate pairs. (1 point each blank)

y = x - 2

x	-2	-1	0	1	2
y					
x,y					

D. Construct a set of axes so that x axes goes (by .5) from –2.5 to 2.5 and the y axis (by 1's) from –6 to 2. (5 points)

Score: /30

Pass: 22/30

Australian Homeschooling #570
Test Your Maths 8

Test 48: Cartesian Planes 2

A. **Complete the table of values for the following equations and list the co-ordinate pairs.** (1 point each blank)

$y = -4x + 2$

x	-2	-1	0	1	2
y					
(x, y)					

B. **Construct a set of axes so that x axes goes (by .5) from –2.5 to 12 and the y axis (by 1's) from -2.5 to 12** (5 points)

C. **Complete the table of values for the following equations and list the co-ordinate pairs.** (1 point each blank)

$y = 2x + 3$

x	-2	-1	0	1	2
y					
(x,y)					

D. **Construct a set of axes so that x axes goes (by .5) from –2.5 to 2.5 and the y axis (by 1's) from –2 to 8.** (5 points)

Score: /30

Pass: 22/30

© Valerie Marett
Coroneos Publications

Australian Homeschooling #570
Test Your Maths 8

Test 49: Average

(1 point each answer)

Answer the questions.

1. The average of two numbers is 46. The difference between them is 20.

    The two numbers are _____ and _____

2. Jenny left at 8.00 am to go to the shops, 5.1 km away.

    She arrived at 9.30 am. Her average speed was _____ km/h.

3. The average of five numbers is 27.

    The five numbers are 42, 17, 23, 30, x.

    X = _____

4. Peter painted 35 model cars in two and a half hours.

    How many cars per hour did he paint?

    _____ cars

5. Alan batted 12, 56, 23, 57, 101, 81 in six innings of cricket.

    His batting average for the six innings was _____ runs.

6. Mary bought nine packets of 2 kg biscuits. She found one of the

    packets half empty. She had _____ kg of biscuits.

7. A bag of flour cost $3 and a bag of rice costs $5.

    (a) Four bags of flour and six bags of rice cost $_____.

    (b) The average cost per bag of the bags purchased is $_____.

8. A bottle of milk costs twice as much as a bottle of juice.

    Three bottles of milk and one bottle of juice cost $14.

    (a) A bottle of milk costs $_____

    (b) A bottle of juice costs $_____

Score: /11

Pass: 8/11

© Valerie Marett
Coroneos Publications

Australian Homeschooling #570
Test Your Maths 8

Test 50: Speed and Rate

(1 point each answer)

Answer the questions.

1. A train left the station at 8 am. It arrived at the next station 24 km away at 8:20am. The average speed of the train is _____ km/hr.

2. Joan walked to the shops 800 metres away. She walks at speed of 4 km per hour. If she left at 9:20 am what time did she arrive?

   _____

3. If a dog runs at a speed of 2 metres per second how far will he travel in 2 minutes? _____ metres

   How far would the dog have travelled if he walked at half the speed?

   _____ metres

4. Peter runs at speed of 7.2 km/hr.

   His speed in metres per second is _____ metres per second.

5. A bus travels 255 km at a speed of 85 km per hour. If it leaves at 11 am what time will it arrive? _____

6. Susan walked her dog 1 1/2 km. She left at 10:38 am. She finished walking at 11:08 am. Her walking speed was _____ km per hour

7. Express 30 km per hour in metres per second

   (Leave the answer as a fraction.) _____ metres per second.

8. Sandy ran 210 metres in 30 seconds.

   Her running speed is _____ metres per second.

Score: __/9   **Pass: 7/9**

© Valerie Marett
Coroneos Publications

Australian Homeschooling #570
Test Your Maths 8

Test 51: Average Speed

(1 point each answer)

Answer the questions.

1.

%15km
60 km/h

Market

*

15km
20 km/h

Jill's Home

)

20km
1 hour

June's Home

Jill travelled by car from home to the market at 60km/h. She then rode her bicycle at 20km/hr to visit June. Jill returned home by ferry which took an hour to complete the journey.

(a) Jill's average speed was _____ km/hr.

(b) The whole trip took _____ hours to complete.

(c) Jill travelled a total of _____ km.

2.

A   B   C

Jim drove for one hour from point A to point B at an average speed of 80 km/h. He then drove for another hour to point C at 100 km/h.

The average speed for the journey was_____ km/h.

3.

A
15 km
B
28 km
C
22 km
D
10 km
E

The line shows David's journey from A to E. He left at 10.15 am and arrived at his destination at 1:15 pm. Calculate his average speed.

Average speed = _____ km/h.

Score: /5   **Pass: 3/5**

Test 52: Speed - Meeting Half-way
(2 points each answer)

Answer the questions.

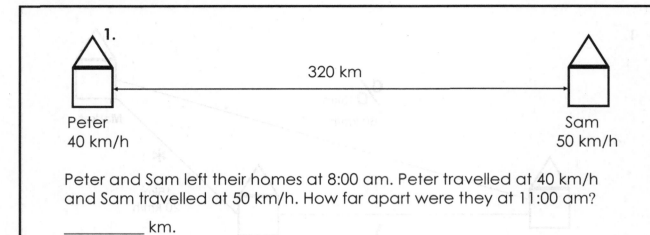

1.

320 km

Peter
40 km/h

Sam
50 km/h

Peter and Sam left their homes at 8:00 am. Peter travelled at 40 km/h and Sam travelled at 50 km/h. How far apart were they at 11:00 am?

_____ km.

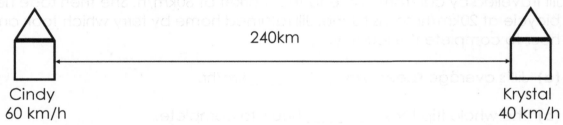

2.

240km

Cindy
60 km/h

Krystal
40 km/h

Cindy left home at 10:00 am. She travelled at an average speed of 60km/h. Krystal left her home at 11:00 am and travelled at an average speed of 40km/h. How far apart were they at 12:30 pm?

_____ km.

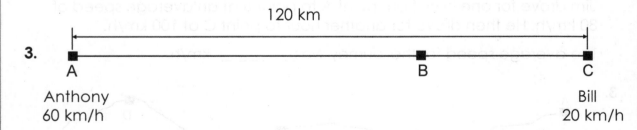

120 km

3.

A   B   C

Anthony
60 km/h

Bill
20 km/h

Anthony and Bill both left home at 10:30 am. Their homes were 120km apart. Anthony travelled at an average speed of 60km/h and Bill at 20km/h.

(a) What time did they meet? _____

(b) How far did Bill travel when they met? _____ km.

Score: ___/8   Pass: 6/8

© Valerie Marett
Coroneos Publications

Australian Homeschooling #570
Test Your Maths 8

Test 53: Square Roots

Find the solution to each problem below. (1 point each)

1. $\sqrt{4}$ _____

2. $\sqrt{16}$ _____

3. $\sqrt{25}$ _____

4. $\sqrt{36}$ _____

5. $\sqrt{81}$ _____

6. $\sqrt{121}$ _____

7. $\sqrt{64}$ _____

8. $\sqrt{49}$ _____

9. $\sqrt{100}$ _____

10. $\sqrt{144}$ _____

11. $\sqrt{169}$ _____

12. $\sqrt{625}$ _____

13. $\sqrt{121} - \sqrt{25}$ _____

14. $\sqrt{36} + \sqrt{25}$ _____

15. $\sqrt{144} - \sqrt{36}$ _____

16. $\sqrt{16} + \sqrt{25}$ _____

17. $\sqrt{49} - \sqrt{16}$ _____

18. $\sqrt{100} + \sqrt{25}$ _____

19. $\sqrt{225} + \sqrt{64}$ _____

20. $\sqrt{169} - \sqrt{144}$ _____

21. $\sqrt{196} - \sqrt{81}$ _____

22. $\sqrt{64} + \sqrt{16}$ _____

23. $16 + \sqrt{100} - 5$ _____

24. $\sqrt{36} + \sqrt{324} - 12$ _____

Score: /24   **Pass: 18/24**

Australian Homeschooling #570
Test Your Maths 8

Test 54: Harder Problems

Simplify each problem below. (1 point each)

1. $ab + 3ab - \sqrt{49} =$ _____

2. $2(bc - 3d) =$ _____

3. $3a + \sqrt{16} = 15$ _____

4. $2a + 3a + 5b =$ _____

5. $\dfrac{2b + 1}{3} + 11 = 12$ _____

6. $2\sqrt{64} + 2a(a + 1) =$ _____

7. $\dfrac{5(a + 2)}{3} = \sqrt{400}$ _____

8. $3(a - 4) - 2(a + 2) =$ _____

9. $-4(p + q) - (p - q) =$ _____

10. $2(m - n) + 3(4m - 2n) =$ _____

11. $6a^3b^2 \div 2ab =$ _____

12. $\dfrac{16cd^4}{cd^4} =$ _____

13. $2a^2c \times 2a \times 4c^4 =$ _____

14. $2a\sqrt{64} - 6ab + b =$ _____

Score: /14

Pass: 10/14

Australian Homeschooling #570
Test Your Maths 8

Test Your Maths 8

Page 3, Test 1
A. Solve the addition & subtraction

1.	5,899	9,330	13,259	14,326	10,913
2.	5,643	4,759	4,953	3,437	3,774
3.	4,906	5,009	5,034	2,664	1,329
4.	16,942	14,121	14,525	15,284	11,714
5.	15,721	1,731	12,643	2,307	952
6.	14,041;	6,172;	14,355;	5,529	3061

B. Answer the problems
1. 9,000
2. 16,000
3. 53,200
4. 23,376

Page 4, Test 2
Long division
1. 156
2. 243
3. 89
4. 422
5. 97
6. 17
7. 37
8. 123
9. 23

Page 5, Test 3: Long multiplication
1. 945
2. 59,768
3. 3,552
4. 27,429
5. 1,326
6. 3,738
7. 3,168
8. 4,896
9. 7,144

Page 6, Test 4: Fractions
A. Reduce to simplest form
1. 3/4
2. 1/7
3. 1/2
4. 1/4
5. 2/3
6. 5/6
7. 1/3
8. 7/8
9. 1/2
10. 9/16
11. 5/12
12. 2/7

B. Equivalent Fractions
1. 1/4
2. 2/3

3. 3/4
4. 1/2
5. 3/5
6. 1/7

C. Express as whole number
1. 2
2. 5
3. 4
4. 17
5. 12
6. 5
7. 5
8. 9
9. 7

D. Mixed Number
1. 7 1/3
2. 4 1/8
3. 7 5/9
4. 8 1/2
5. 3 3/4
6. 21 3/4

Page 7, Test 5: Addition of Fractions
A. Add the following fractions
1. 1
2. 8/9
3. 9/10
4. 1 1/12 or 13/12
5. 1 1/14 or 15/14
6. 3 1/2 or 21/6
7. 13/15
8. 2 5/8

B. Add the following mixed numbers
1. 6 1/3
2. 4 19/33
3. 7 1/35
4. 20 11/12
5. 5 47/90
6. 7 2/15
7. 6 2/7
8. 10 3/4

Page 8, Test 6: Subtraction of Fractions
A. Subtract the following fractions
1. 1/36
2. 61/99
3. 9/40
4. 1/12
5. 21/40
6. 1
7. 2 1/5 or 22/10
8. 1/9

B. Subtract the following mixed fractions
1. 1 5/6
2. 1 5/12

Australian Homeschooling #570
Test Your Maths 8

Test Your Maths 8

3. 1 5/12
4. 3/8
5. 2 1/8
6. 7 1/6
7. 6 5/6
8. 2 5/27

Page 9, Test 7: Addition and Subtraction of Fractions
A. Calculate the following fractions
1. 1 2/3
2. 143/180
3. 4/5
4. 11/18
5. 1 11/42
6. 1 1/12
7. 3/16
8. 28/75

B. Calculate the following mixed fractions
1. 13
2. 69 53/54
3. 10 3/4
4. 55 41/42

Page 10, Test 8: Multiplication of Fractions
1. 1/3
2. 5/99
3. 9/35
4. 5/24
5. 1/15
6. 5/6
7. 1 2/5
8. 24 3/4
9. 3 3/4
10. 1 1/2
11. 2
12. 9/35
13. 2 2/3
14. 3/16

Page 11, Test 9: Division of Fractions
1. 1 3/5
2. 3
3. 2
4. 1/12
5. 1 5/6
6. 4/7
7. 1 5/9
8. 7/33
9. 4 9/10
10. 1 1/6
11. 3
12. 2
13. 1/8
14. 2 5/8

Page 12, Test 10: Fraction problems
1. $360
2. $320
3. 30
4. 1000 sheep   1500 goats
5. 90 yellow   20 green

Page 13, Test 11:
Percentages of a Number; Fractions to a Percentage; Percentage to a Fraction

A. 1. 30
2. 8
3. 16
4. 14
5. 10
6. 200
7. 1
8. 147
9. 100
10. 12

B. 1. 150%
2. 233%
3. 25%
4. 60%
5. 80%
6. 75%
7. 650%
8. 12½% or 12.5%
9. 460%
10. 37½% or 37.5%

C. 1. 1/4
2. 2/5
3. 4/5
4. 2 1/4
5. 1/2
6. !1/2
7. 1/8
8. 1
9. 1/10
10. 0

Page 14, Test 12: Percentage problems
1. 225   270
2. 34
3. 4
4. 65
5. 72   30%
6. 89%
7. 80kg
8. 60%

Test Your Maths 8

Page 15, Test 13:
More percentage problems
1. $100   33.3%
2. $780
3. 6
4. **(a)** $196
   (b) $98
   (c) $84
   (d) $42
5. $50
6. **(a)** 25%
   (b) 12
   (c) 16
   (d) 8
   (e) 12

   (b) $98
   (c) $84
   (d) $42

Page 16, Test 14: Decimals
A. 1. 3.5
   2. 4.006
   3. 640.2
   4. 2,500.28
   5. 2.632
B. 1. 7.313
   2. 751.731
   3. 8.90467
   4. 268.00426
   5. 0.507
   6. 105.358
   7. 0.529
   8. 1.8
   9. 0.15
   10. 4.2

Page 17, Test 15
Adding and Subtracting Decimals
A. Fill in the blanks
1. 3.8
2. 2.76
3. 5.9
4. 2.6
5. 1.94
6. 3.16
7. 2.78
8. 11.56

B. Complete the following
1. 0.74
2. 0.61
3. 3.19
4. 5.74
5. 65.03

6. 8.36
C. Fill in missing number
1. 0
2. 5
3. 7
4. 4

Page 18, Test 16
Word Problems—Decimals
N.B. All answers must be labeled, e.g., kg, litres, $ etc
1. $54.16
2. 51.09kg
3. $14.87
4. 93.05kg
5. 12.695 kg
6. 2.61 litres

Page 19, Test 17
More Decimals
A. 1. 110
   2. 3,296
   3. 145,600
   4. 0.000,02
   5. 0.046
   6. 18,200
   7. 0.036
   8. 100
B. 1. 500 gm
   2. 0.45 kg
   3. 400 ml
   4. 2.357 km
   5. 2.5 mm
   6. 64,900 cents
   7. 45,589 mm
   8. 547.2 mm
C. 1. 7.49
   2. 0.04
   3. 2,020
   4. 935.22
   5. 63.75
   6. 2,548,502.68
   7. 0.18
   8. 85.3

Page 20, Test 18
Multiplying Decimals
A. Find the value
1. $4
2. $0.12
3. $4.50
4. $5.40
5. $10.80
6. $51.45
7. 13.86
8. 76.2

Test Your Maths 8

9. 302.4
10. 6.65
11. 51.4
12. 446.24

B. Multiply
1. 1
2. 0.24
3. 22.05
4. 139.32
5. 70.77
6. 23.01
7. 388.2
8. 11.7
9. 308.07
10. 123.15
11. 3.2
12. 18.75

Page 21, Test 19
Division of Decimals
1. 3.75
2. 0.59
3. 1.76
4. 1.42
5. 2.4
6. 0.04
7. 0.85
8. 0.59
9. 0.71
10. 0.802
11. 0.75
12. 2.91
13. 0.67

Page 22, Test 20
Word Problems—Multiplication & Division
1. 2.5 kg
2. $74.50
3. 55 bags
4. 0.8 litres
5. 1.6kg each
6. $22.20 $164.95

Page 23, Test 21
A. Convert the decimal number to a fraction.
1. 3 1/4
2. 7/8
3. 47 4/5
4. 1/100
5. 17 3/4
6. 10 1/5
7. 49 3/5
8. 30 7/20
9. 57 17/20
10. 47 7/10

11. 9/2500
12. 9,587 31/250

B. Fractions to a Decimal Number
1. 89.28
2. 4.375
3. 2398.05
4. 0.5
5. 2.75
6. 0.875
7. 37.75
8. 7024.33
9. 857.5
10. 0.25
11. 200,347.76
12. 347,469.375

Page 24, Test 22
A. Round the number to two decimal places
1. 76.97
2. 0.27
3. 0.26
4. 0.08
5. 4,892.54
6. 11.11
7. 87.68
8. 4.00

B. Convert the decimal number to a percentage
1. 50%
2. 137%
3. 286.5%
4. 1690%
5. 5%
6. 1020%
7. 4.96%
8. 30.35%

C. Convert the fraction to a percentage
1. 33.33%
2. 75%
3. 250%
4. 87.5%
5. 305%
6. 26%
7. 28%
8. 336%

Page 25, Test 23
A. Multiply the following.
1. 270.16
2. 150
3. 1.2
4. 24
5. 820
6. 0.25
7. 0.008
8. 3.365

© Valerie Marett
CORONEOS PUBLICATIONS

Australian Homeschooling #570
Test Your Maths 8

9. 23
10. 9.12
11. 3.6
12. 10.8
13. 0.25
14. 145.2
15. 10,000
16. 1,000,000

C. Divide the following.
1. 560
2. 640
3. 0.02
4. 0.5
5. 8
6. 1.2
7. 1.2
8. 0.01
9. 6938
10. 2.514
11. 1.056
12. 9548.7
13. 5.236
14. 8979.75

Page 26, Test 24
Factors and multiples
A. 1. 2 x 3 x 3
   2. 2 x 2 x 3
   3. 2 x 3 x 5 x 5
   4. 2 x 2 x 2 x 2 x 2 x 3
   5. 2 x 2 x 2 x 2 x 3 x 3
   6. 3 x 3 x 5 x 5
   7. 2 x 3 x 3 x 7
   8. 3 x 3 x 3 x 37

B. 1. 16   **2.** 18
   3. 3   **4.** 42

C. 1. 5
   2. 14
   3. 1, 2, 3
   4. 2, 2, 2, 5, 5
   5. 32, 128, 1024
   6. 1, 3, 9, 21
   7. 9
   8. 11

Page 27, Test 25
A. All Common Factors
   1. 1, 2, 4, 8, 12, 24
   2. 1, 2, 11, 22
   3. 1, 2, 7, 14
   4. 1, 3, 9

B. Highest common factor (HCF)
1. 6
2. 18
3. 2
4. 16
5. 9
6. 15
7. 48
8. 56

A. Lowest common multiple (LCM)
   1. 26
   2. 56
   3. 108
   4. 12
   5. 150
   6. 56
   7. 10
   8. 30

B. HCF/ LCM
   1. 8   24
   2. 3   72
   3. 16   128

Page 28, Test 26
Index notation
A. 1. $2^5 \times 3^1$
   2. 2^8
   3. $5^1 \times 3^2 \times 7^1$
   4. $2^3 \times 3^3$
   5. $2^3 \times 5^2 \times 11^1$
   6. $2^7 \times 5^7$

B. 1. 16
   2. 100
   3. 243
   4. 127
   5. 21
   6. 0

C. 1. 3^2
   2. 7^3
   3. 3^3
   4. 2^3
   5. 7^2
   6. 5^2

D. 1. $2^4 \times 3$
   2. 3^3
   3. $3^4 \times 7^3$
   4. 3^1
   5. $6^1 \times 10^6$
   6. 2^4
   7. 3^1
   8. 2^3

Page 29, Test 27
Ratios
A. Simplest ratio
1. 3:2
2. 2:3
3. 4:5
4. 1:2
5. 7:2
6. 3:1

B. Answer the questions
1. 3:10
2. 5:18
3. 5:9
4. 5:3
5. 20kg
6. 4:1
7. 1:4
8. 8 years old
9. 6 years

Page 30, Test 28
Relationship between Ratios and Fractions
1. (a) 3/16
   (b) 3/8
   (c) 7/16
   (d) 12
   (e) 24
   (f) 28
2. $20
3. 9
4. 12   60
5. (a) 12
   (b) 21
   (c) 6
6. (a) 16
   (b) 44
   (c) 64
   (d) 12

Page 31, Test 29
Perimeter
1. 40cm
2. 96cm
3. 24m
4. 32.5cm
5. 2900mm
6. 350mm
7. 455m
8. 52m
9. 57m

Page 32, Test 30
Area of a triangle
1. 24cm^2
2. 216cm^2

3. 10cm^2
4. 18cm^2
5. 100cm^2
6. 135cm^2
7. 65cm^2
8. 49cm^2

Page 33, Test 31
Area of composite figures
1. 144mm^2
2. 144cm^2
3. 9,000mm^2
4. 135mm^2
5. 192m^2
6. 148.5cm^2
7. 208m^2
8. 72m^2

Page 34, Test 32
Volume
1. 400ml
2. 720ml
3. 100mm
4. 10mm

Page 35, Test 33
Calculating length, breadth and height
1. 3m
2. 40m
3. 60m
4. 5m

Page 36,Test 34
Circles - Circumference
1. 125.6 mm
2. 9.42 metres
3. (a) 21 metres
   (b) 10½ metres
4. (a) 3 metres
   (b) 6 metres
   (c) 18.84 metres
5. 11 metres

Page 37,Test 35
Circles - Area
1. 154 cm^2
2. 12.56 cm^2
3. (a) 78.5 m^2
   (b) 21.5 m^2
   (c) 15.7 m
4. ¾n m^2

Page 38, Test 36
Algebra—finding a value
A. Find the value of x
1. 4
2. 6

3. 8
4. 6
5. 4
6. 200
7. 3
8. 12
9. 4
10. 3

B. Find the value of x
1. 12
2. 1
3. 11
4. 2
5. 2
6. 400
7. 48
8. 20
9. 6
10. 3

Page 39, Test 37
Algebraic substitution
A. 1. 135
2. 21
3. 33
4. 49
5. 66
6. 287
B 1. 168
2. 19
3. 25
4. 34
5. 46
6. 9
7. 120
8. 64
9. 84
10. 72

Page 40, Test 38
Algebraic Simplification
1. $13a + 21$
2. $10x + 8$
3. $2s + 2$
4. $3a^2 + 6ab$
5. $3ht$
6. $9a + 17b$
7. $-2b + 2c$
8. $-5p$
9. $12x - 6y - 18$
10. $28 + 16p - 17q$

Page 41, Test 39
Algebraic Simplification 2
1. $2b$

2. $\dfrac{1}{3d}$

3. $\dfrac{y}{3}$

4. $2p$
5. a

6. $\dfrac{3pq}{4}$

7. $\dfrac{37s}{30}$

8. $\dfrac{3x + 10}{10}$

Page 42, Test 40
Algebraic Simplification 3
1. a

2. $\dfrac{t}{2r}$

3. p
4. y
5. $14a$

6. $\dfrac{7d}{4}$

7. nq
8. $6p$

Page 43, Test 41
Algebra: Expanding Brackets
1. $a^{12}b^8$
2. $4a^6b^4$
3. $12^3a^6b^9$ or $1728a^6b^9$
4. $25a^4b^6c^8$

5. $\dfrac{a^4}{b^6}$

6. $\dfrac{8a^{12}}{b^3c^6}$

7. $\dfrac{36a^6b^2}{4c^8}$

Page 44, Test 42
Geometry
1. $135°$
2. $45°$
3. $40°$
4. $330°$
5. $35°$
6. $120°$

Page 45, Test 43
Triangles and parallelograms
1. $70°$
2. $25°$
3. $120°$
4. $37°$
5. $36°$
6. $78°$ $37°$ $143°$

Page 46, Test 44
Triangles and parallelograms
1. 315°
2. 30°   120°
3. 234°
4. 15°
5. 33°
6. 25°

Page 47, Test 45
A. Bar graph
(see page 65)
B. Answer questions from graph
1. Darwin 34°C
2. Hobart 17°C or 18°C
(both acceptable)
3. Melbourne   Canberra
4. four
5. east coast

Page 48, Test 46
A. Pie graph
(see page 65)
B. Answer questions from the pie graph
1. swimming   softball
2. soccer
3. 1,716 played soccer
4. 26.08%
5. Softball, Martial Arts, Aerobics   13%

Page 49, Test 47

A. $y = 3x$

x	-2	-1	0	1	2
y	-6	-3	0	3	6
(x,y)	-2,-6	-1,-3	0,0	1,3	2,6

B. Cartesian graph
(See page 65)

C. $y = x - 2$

x	-2	-1	0	1	2
y	-4	-3	-2	-1	0
x,y	-2,-4	-1,3	0,-2	1,-1	2,0

D. Cartesian Graph
(See page 66)

Page 50, Test 48
A. $y = -4x + 2$

x	-2	-1	0	1	2
y	-6	6	2	-2	-6
(x, y)	-2,10	-1,6	0,2	,-2	2,-6

B. Cartesian graph
(See page 66)

C. $y = 2x + 3$

x	-2	-1	0	1	2
y	-1	1	3	5	7
(x, y)	-2,-1	-1,1	0,3	1,5	2,7

D. Cartesian graph
(See page 65).

Page 51, Test 49
Average
1. 20, 26
2. 3.4 km/h
3. 23
4. 14 cars
5. 55
6. 17 kg
7. **(a)** $42
   (b) $4.20
8. **(a)** $4
   (b) $2

Page 52, Test 50
Speed and rate
1. 72 km/h
2. 9.32 am
3. 240 m   120 m
4. 0.12 m/s or 120m
5. 2 pm
6. 3 km/h
7. 500 m/s
8. 70 m/s

Page 53, Test 51
Average speed
1. **(a)** 33.3 km/h
   (b) 2 hours
   (c) 50 km
2. 90 km/h
3. 25 km/h

Australian Homeschooling #570
Test Your Maths 8

Page 54, Test 52
Speed - meeting halfway
1. 50km
2.   30km
3. **(a)** 12 pm
   (b) 30 km

Page 55, Test 53
Square Roots
1. 2
2. 4
3, 5
4. 6
5. 9
6. 11
7. 8
8. 7
9. 10
10. 12
11. 13
12. 25
13. 6
14. 11
15. 6
16. 9
17. 3
18. 15
19. 23
20. 1
21. 5
22. 12
23. 11
24. 12

Page 56, Test 54
Harder Problems
1. $4ab - 7$
2. $2bc - 6d$
3. $a = 11/3$
4. $5a + 5b$
5. $b = 1$
6. $16 + 2a^2 + 2a$
7. $a = 10$
8. $a - 8$
9. $-5p - 3q$
10. $14m - 8n$
11. $3a^2b$
12. 16
13. $16a^3c^5$
14. $16a - 6ab + b$

Page 47, Test 45
A.   Bar graph

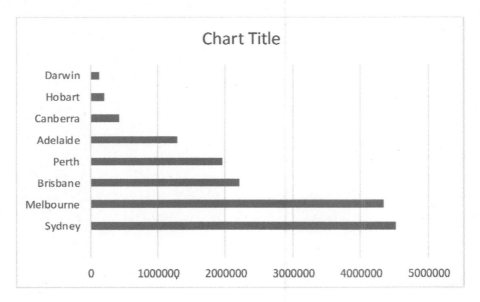

Page 48, Test 46
A. Pie graph

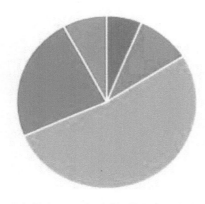

cats   dogs   fish   birds   other

Page 49, Test 47   **B. plot graph**

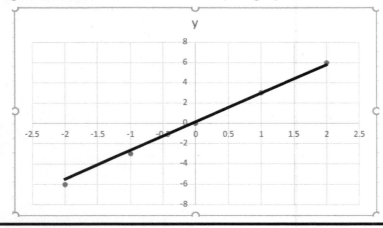

Test Your Maths 8

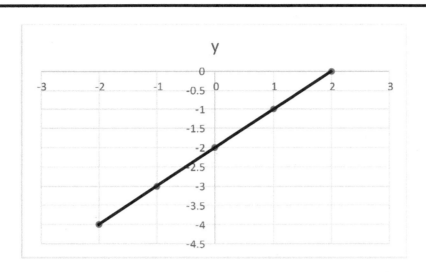

Page 49, Test 47
D. plot graph

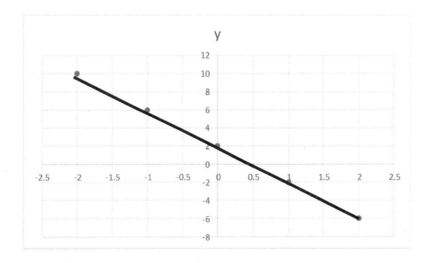

Page 50, Test 48
B. plot graph

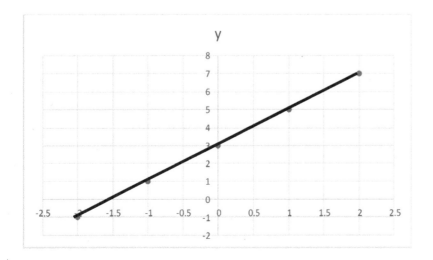

Page 50, Test 48
D. plot graph